EXPLORING

Biblical Essentials Everyone Should Know

Tatyana Zhuk

www.SavedHome.com

Copyright © 2019 by Tatyana Zhuk. All rights reserved. No part of this book may be reproduced in any manner without written permission except in the case of brief quotations included in critical articles and reviews. For information, please contact the author.
Savedhome.com

Scripture taken from the New King James Version®. Copyright © 1982 by Thomas Nelson. Used by permission. All rights reserved.

ISBN 978-0-578-41677-9

Editors
Irina Kobrya;
Dina Homeier;
Viktor Dorofeyev;
Alison Roeser;
Julie Teleten.

Photography
Olga Strizheus

Illustrations taken of:
Family and friends

Illustrations of creatures are taken from:
Freeimages.com

Illustrations Edited by:
Tatyana Zhuk via Cartoon Face & Adobe Draw app

This book is also available in Russian language and may be available in other languages in the future.

Contents

Acknowledgments

A Word to Parents

TO KNOW GOD 2

GOD CANNOT BE SEEN 4

GOD IS EVERYWHERE AND KNOWS EVERYTHING 6

GOD IS UNITED, AND GOD IS HOLY ..8

GOD IS ALMIGHTY 10

GOD IS FAITHFUL 12

GOD HAS MANY NAMES 14

GOD MADE ALL THINGS GOOD 16

GOD MADE US 18

SIN CAME INTO THE WORLD 20

A SINNER 22

THE LAW 24

THE WAGES OF SIN IS ETERNAL DEATH 26

GOD TAKES CARE OF US 28

JESUS CAME FROM HEAVEN 30

JESUS OBEYED GOD 32

JESUS TAUGHT PEOPLE 34

JESUS RULES OVER SICKNESS AND DEATH. HE FORGIVES SIN 36

JESUS DIED FOR YOU 38

JESUS LIVES AGAIN 40

JESUS PRAYS FOR YOU 42

THE HOLY SPIRIT 44

THE WORK OF THE HOLY SPIRIT 46

THE GIFTS AND THE FRUIT OF THE SPIRIT 48

BEING FILLED WITH THE HOLY SPIRIT 50

BECOMING CHILD OF GOD 52

SALVATION 54

NEW CREATION 56

NEW LIFE 58

SPIRITUAL GROWTH 60

TELLING OTHERS ABOUT JESUS 62

PRAYER 64

THE BIBLE 66

UNDERSTANDING THE BIBLE 68

SPIRITUAL ARMOR 70

THE CHURCH 72

YOUR SPIRITUAL FAMILY 74

THE CHURCH'S ASSIGNMENT 76

BAPTISM 78

THE LORD'S SUPPER 80

THE END TIMES 82

IF I DIE 84

HEAVEN 86

HELL 88

THE SECOND COMING OF JESUS 90

Acknowledgments

Exploring Biblical Essentials Everyone Should Know is the result of personal prayers for our children. They have inspired this long journey of studying the Word of God and committing it to paper in a way they could understand and live by.

We are deeply grateful for pastors, parents and individuals who came along and supported this material, making it available to the public. Above all, we cannot be thankful enough to our God, who reveals Himself so even a small child can grasp His truth.

A Word to Parents

This book is intended to be used as a guide by parents who desire to tell their little ones about the great God who created us and about the essential teaching of life. Material such as this should be read slowly, so the child's mind can accept and store it in his or her heart. You will find that some truths are elementary while others are beyond our ability to grasp, and that's ok; they can be left as secrets. Our job is to help our child develop God's worldview. This will equip children to love and choose what is best on their own.

To help make this reading most meaningful, we encourage you to set aside a special time, such as during family devotions in the morning, and/or at bedtime.

With each lesson, we introduce a new word for a child to understand and learn.

All scripture quotations are taken from the Holy Bible: New Kings James Version (NKJV). We have included questions to help parents understand their child's thinking and for the child to apply the teachings to his or her life.

Prayers are suggested at the end of each lesson. They are a precious way of watering the seed that has just been sown into the child's heart.

We pray that this material will serve you and your family as you read it to your child. May it be a blessing everywhere it is used.

"And this I pray, that your love may abound still more and more in knowledge and all discernment, that you may approve the things that are excellent, that you may be sincere and without offense till the day of Christ,"
Philippians 1:9-10

1

TO KNOW GOD

"Seek the Lord while He may be found,
call upon Him while He is near."
Isaiah 55:6

Have you tried making something like a castle out of the sand, a tower out of Lego blocks, or an animal out of Play-Doh? Did that make you feel happy? You know someone also made the world, the sky, plants, stars, the moon, the sun, the birds that fly, fish that swim, and all the animals. Everything you see was made by God! No one created God; He has always been there before anything else ever was. God has also made you, and you belong to Him. Everything in the universe belongs to God, and He cares about everything He created. That's why He is very important. He can see you, hear you, and help you.

Do you think you should know Him? Yes! The most important thing in the whole world is to know God personally. Knowing God should be your life's main goal. That's because everything you understand about God will shape your whole life. Do you want to have joy and do the right thing? Would you like to know the truth about yourself and this world? You need to know what God has to say about it all; then, you can make the right choices and have the right feelings about everything.

Did you know that every house is only as strong as its foundation? The foundation is the base that is at the very bottom of the house; it is what the house is built on. What you build your life on also matters! Your life will only be as good as your foundation. If your foundation is made up of opinions and feelings, then it has a very weak foundation. That's because sometimes our opinions and feelings are wrong. That's like building a house on jiggly Jell-O! It will not be sturdy. But, if your life's foundation is based on what the Bible teaches, you will have a very strong foundation like cement. In fact, it is the only foundation that will last. When your life is based on what the Bible teaches, it will reach the goodness that God desires for your life. So, set your heart, mind and your eyes on God's Word, the Bible.

New word: Foundation – the base of a building, it holds the heavy load of the building.

Questions to ask:
1. To whom does everything belong?
2. What should be your life's main goal?
3. Why is it important to have a good foundation for your life?

Read and discuss
Matthew 7:24-29 (Build on the Rock),
Deuteronomy 6:1-9 (Through Moses, God tells the Israelites to love God before they enter the Promised Land).

Let's pray and thank God for all of the things He created. Let's ask Him to help you know Him and to be the strong foundation of your life.

Dear God, thank You for being the Creator of everything in the universe! Thank You for creating me and the people around me. Please help me build my life on Your Word by following Your direction so that my life can be good and strong. Amen.

2
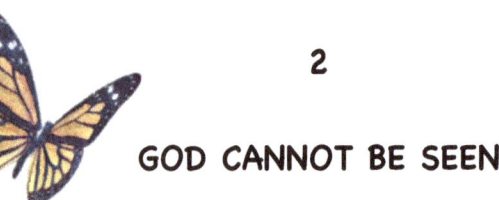
GOD CANNOT BE SEEN

"No one has seen God at any time. If we love one another,
God abides in us, and His love has been perfected in us."
1 John 4:12

No person has ever seen God. You cannot see God because He is a spirit. You have a body, and inside of it is your spirit. Your spirit is what gives life to your body. The Bible says that the body without the spirit is dead. It is like a radio that needs electricity in order to work. You cannot see your spirit; you see only your body. God does not have a body like you, and that is why you do not see Him.

Even though you cannot see God, you know that there is a God because you can see the things He has made, like the flowers and the birds. He is always working in your life. At times, He can help you fix a bad relationship or help you break a bad habit. When you are scared or worried, He can give you peace. God is just as real as you are even when you cannot see Him! He also has wishes, interests and plans like you have.

You can talk to God through prayer. He also may speak to you in several ways. His Spirit can softly say something good into your heart and tell you not to be afraid or to be careful in a certain situation. God's Spirit can tell you not to be bad and listen to your mom and dad. He can show something to you through a dream. He can be telling you something through other people like your good friends, parents, and people at church. God also talks to you through His book. Long ago, God told a few chosen men to write down His words, and so they made a big book that we now call the Bible. God talks to you when you read the Bible.

New word: Spirit – the invisible part of a person, it lives on even after physical death.

Questions to ask:
1. Has anyone seen God?
2. Why can't you see God?
3. How do you know that there is a God?
4. Can you talk to God? May God speak to you?

Read and discuss
Exodus 33:12-23 (God passes by Moses),
1 Samuel 3:1-10 (God speaks to little boy Samuel).

Let's thank God for making Himself known.
Dear God, even though we cannot see You with our eyes, thank You for letting us know You through creation, the Holy Spirit, and the Bible. Thank You for always wanting to talk to us. Amen.

GOD IS EVERYWHERE AND KNOWS EVERYTHING

"Can anyone hide himself in secret places, so I shall not see him?" says the Lord; "Do I not fill heaven and earth?" says the Lord."
Jeremiah 23:24

God is everywhere at the same time! You cannot see Him, but He is here, and He is also over there. You are never alone because God is everywhere, and He always sees you. He hears what you say and watches what you do even when no people are around. Sometimes you will feel like you are all alone, but those feelings are not true, because God is always very near. There is nothing too small or too big that His presence cannot reach. His presence may not be noticed in the same way at the same time to people everywhere, but He fills all things with His presence. All things were created through Him and for Him and in Him all things exist.

God knows everything! He knows how many stars there are in heaven. He even knows what you think and what you want. That is because He lives outside of time and existed before anything else. He knows what happened yesterday and what will happen tomorrow and the day after tomorrow. God is very great. He is bigger than any distance, and He knows all things. Nothing can surprise God.

New word: Distance – the amount of space between two things or people.

Questions to ask:
1. Are you ever alone?
2. What does God know?
3. Does anything surprise God?

Read and discuss
Jonah 1:1-17 (Jonah wanted to hide from the Lord),
Psalms 139:1-18 (God's perfect knowledge of man).

Let's thank God that He is everywhere.
Dear God, thank You for always being with us everywhere and all the time so that we don't have to be alone or afraid, even at night. No one else is like You! Help us to say and do what You want because You watch over us, and no one can hide anything from You. Amen.

4

GOD IS UNITED, AND GOD IS HOLY

*"For there are three that bear witness in heaven:
the Father, the Word, and the Holy Spirit; and these three are one."*
1 John 5:7

God is very great, and we cannot understand, explain or know everything about Him. Bible says that our God comes to us in three different Persons: The Father, the Son, and the Holy Spirit. For example, a family has a dad, a mom, and a child. They are all very different people, but they all make one family. They look different; they do different things; and they can make different choices. But, they are still one family. Similarly, God's three Persons are described in the Bible. God the Father lives in heaven. He loved the world and gave His only Son, so that whoever believes in His Son shall not perish but have eternal life. Jesus is God the Son who came down to earth and took on a human form. He died for our sins on the cross to save us. God the Holy Spirit lives in the hearts of those who believe in Jesus and have received Him into their lives. While the Father and the Son are in heaven, the Holy Spirit is on earth with us. He helps believers go through difficulties on earth to get to heaven. These three are united. God is holy because He is separated from evil. Holy means that God is very clean and pure. God always does things right. He never does wrong or evil; He never sins. There is nothing wrong about Him. He is like a very, very bright shining light.

New word: United – joined together for a common purpose.

Questions to ask:
1. Can we understand everything about God?
2. Are the Father, the Son, and the Holy Spirit united?
3. Does God ever do any wrong?

Read and discuss
Matthew 3:13-17 (John baptizes Jesus),
Isaiah 6:1-5 (Isaiah sees angels).

Let's pray and thank God that He is our true God.
Dear God, thank You for being holy. Thank You for loving us even though You are so good, and we are not. Please teach me to be good and holy like You. Amen.

5

GOD IS ALMIGHTY

"When Abram was ninety-nine years old, the Lord appeared to Abram and said to him, "I am Almighty God; walk before Me and be blameless."
Genesis 17:1

God is Almighty, which means He can do anything He wants. He can heal, do miracles, and answer prayers all around the world at the same time. He is very powerful, and He uses His power to create and love His creation. God has no evil therefore, everything He does is good and right! God is the ruler of everything and everybody. He does not have to ask or depend on anyone, and He doesn't have to explain His choices to anyone. He has everything in His hands. He is always in control even when you make your own choices! That might be hard to understand, but that's ok. Some things you don't need to understand right now; God can reveal them to you later. God is so much bigger and greater than you and I. He is bigger than any situation, bigger than any sickness, any storm, any problem, and any living thing. God is greater than the universe! Hebrews 3:3-4 tells us that "He who built the house has more honor than the house. For every house is built by someone, but He who built all things is God." God is greater than all the things that He has made; He is greater than His deeds.

New word: In control – able to direct or influence.

Questions to ask:
1. Can God do anything He wants?
2. Who is always in control of everything that happens or will happen?
3. Can any situation be bigger than God?

Read and discuss
Daniel 4:28-37 (A powerful king Nebuchadnezzar praises God),
Exodus 8:1-32 (God performs plagues on Egypt).

Let's pray and thank God that we belong to Him.
Dear God, You are the most powerful in the world, and You can control everything. Thank You for being our Almighty God and for loving us. Amen.

6

GOD IS FAITHFUL

"Let us hold fast the confession of our hope without wavering, for He who promised is faithful."
Hebrews 10:23

God is faithful. Have you promised your dad or mom to be good and that you would listen to them, but then you forgot or weren't able to do it? This means you were not able to keep your promise. But, God never breaks a promise! His promises are firm because He is faithful. He never forgets His promises either, even after many years have passed.

If God promises something, He will always fulfill it. Long ago there was an old man Abram who wanted a child but couldn't have one. God made a promise to Abram to give him many descendants. God kept His promise! We can find this story in the Bible in Genesis chapter 15.

Abram had to wait patiently for many years. God's promise wasn't fulfilled right away. There are many things that God has promised you too, and He still keeps His promises today. You can trust God because He is not like people who sometimes break their promises; He is always faithful.

New word: Promise – a statement that you will definitely do something or that something will definitely happen.

Questions to ask:
1. Does God ever forget?
2. Was God's promise to Abram fulfilled right away?
3. Does God still keep His promises today?

Read and discuss
Genesis 9:8-17 (God's promise to Noah),
Joshua 3:14-17; 21:43-45 (Israelites crossing the Jordan River into the land that God promised).

People may break their promises very often, but let's pray and thank God because He always keeps His wonderful promises.

Dear God, thank You for always doing what You say. Help us wait for Your answer and trust You. Amen.

7

GOD HAS MANY NAMES

"*"I am the Alpha and the Omega, the Beginning and the End," says the Lord, "who is and who was and who is to come, the Almighty."*"
Revelation 1:8

God has many names. Everybody and everything have a name, even cars, stores, and flowers. Their name tells us about who they are. It is how they are known or spoken to. God has more than one name. Sometimes, we call Him Father. Sometimes, we call Him Helper, Healer, Provider or Savior. One other wonderful name of God is I AM. This name means that God has always been around, and He will never end. This name also means that He will never change. God has many names because each name describes the wonderful character God has.

You should use His name carefully when you talk to Him and when you talk about Him to others. God's name is to be used with respect and honor because God is very wonderful and holy. His name is not to be emptied of honor or meaning. So, never say God's name just for fun; it is to be treated as special.

New word: Special – better, more important, or different from what is usual.

Questions to ask:
1. How many names does God have?
2. What does a name tell us about a person?
3. Should you use God's name carefully?

Read and discuss
Exodus 3:1-4, 10-14 (The burning bush).

14

Let's thank God in prayer for His great names.
Dear God, thank You for all of the wonderful names You have.
Thank you for always being around and never changing.
Please help me guard my mouth and only say Your name with honor and love.
Amen.

8

GOD MADE ALL THINGS GOOD

"In the beginning God created the heaven and the earth."
Genesis 1:1

There are many wonderful things all around you: the big blue sky and white clouds; all kinds of beautiful flowers, butterflies, and bugs; different animals and birds. Where did these things come from? Bible tells us that God made all things. Long ago, there was no sky, no trees, no animals, and no people; only God was there. One time, He began to make all the wonderful things we see. God only spoke a word, and the things He said were created out of nothing, just by His word! For example, God said, "Let there be light," and light appeared.

Everything He made was good, and He did it in the correct order. First, He created the light, then the sky, water, land, plants, and animals. God didn't create all this because He had to; He simply wanted to, and He enjoyed creating. When God finished making the world, He didn't just leave it to work on its own somehow. Bible tells us many times that God takes care of it continually! He is like the glue that holds the entire universe together. Without Him, it would all fall apart. God also takes care of you! He does so by giving you parents and others to look after you and help you. But, even if your mom or dad can't be around, God is always there for you.

New word: World – the earth, together with all of its countries, people, and nature.

Questions to ask:
1. Who made the sky, trees and animals?
2. How did God make all these things?
3. Did God create anything bad?

Read and discuss
Genesis 1:1-25 (Creation).

Let's pray and thank God for making all things good and beautiful just by speaking the word.

Dear God, You are very good and powerful. Thank You for making this world so creatively and with love. Thank You for always doing what is best for everyone. Amen.

9

GOD MADE US

"God created man in his own image;
in the image of God He created him; male and female He created them."
Genesis 1:27

There are many people on this earth. Where did all these people come from? After God made the beautiful earth, He made the first man out of dust in His own image. God gave this man a wonderful body, feelings, and a mind, so he could think. God called that man Adam. When Adam was in deep sleep, God took a rib out of his side and made a woman out of it. When Adam awoke, God brought this beautiful woman to him. Adam called her Eve. Adam loved Eve, and over time they had many children, both boys and girls. The children grew up, they married, and also had children. Soon, many people were living on this earth.

God did not make Adam and Eve because He was lonely. He already had a perfect relationship with God the Son and God the Holy Spirit. God created Adam and Eve, so they could have a relationship with Him and see His glory. That is how good, loving and caring God is.

God wants to have a personal relationship with you too! He is interested in every detail of your life: like what you wear, what you eat, and how you spend your day. All boys and girls are created in His image no matter what their skin color is, what country they live in, or what language they speak. King David recognized that God created him. He wrote about it in Psalm 139:13-18, "For You formed my inward parts; You covered me in my mother's womb. I will praise You, for I am fearfully and wonderfully made; marvelous are Your works, and that my soul knows very well. My frame was not hidden from You, when I was made in secret, and skillfully wrought in the lowest parts of the earth. Your eyes saw my substance, being yet unformed. And in Your book they all were written, the days fashioned for me, when as yet there were none of them. How precious also are Your thoughts of me, O God! How great is the sum of them! If I should count them, they would be more in number than the sand; when I awake, I am still with You." God has created you for His purpose too; you are not an accident. You can say those words together with King David and thank God for making you!

New word: Image – a representation of how someone or something looks.

Questions to ask:
1. Who were the first people that God made?
2. Why did God make Adam and Eve?
3. In whose image are all boys and girls created?

Read and discuss
Genesis 1:26-28; 2:7-8, 21-23 (God created male and female).

Let's thank God for wonderfully making you in His image.

Dear God, thank You for making me in Your image. Thank You for the body that I live in, for my heart that I feel with, and for my mind that I can know You. Thank You for my spirit that will live forever with You. Amen.

10

SIN CAME INTO THE WORLD

"Through one man sin entered the world, and death through sin, and thus death spread to all men, because all sinned."
Romans 5:12

When God was making the world, everything was so good and beautiful. Today, many things are not good anymore, and people are often not happy. That is because sin has come into the world. Bible tells us that Adam and Eve first lived in a beautiful garden that God made. There were many delicious fruits to eat, but there was one tree in the garden that God told Adam and Eve not to eat from because they would die.

Now, God has an enemy. His name is Satan; he hates God and His creation. Satan is an angel who fell from heaven because of pride. He was jealous of God and wanted to be greater than God. Satan is a real spiritual being, not just an idea, who is constantly working against God and those who love God. Satan heard what God told Adam about the forbidden tree, and Satan lied to Eve to get her to eat the fruit and disobey God. Adam and Eve both ate the fruit that God did not allow, and that was their first sin. Sin came into the world because Adam and Eve disobeyed God. And bad things began to happen even to good people. People are being killed in crimes and in wars, many are starving, and are being badly hurt/abused. Unwanted things happen to innocent people all around the world. This first sin has changed the history for all mankind. People became mean and selfish on the inside, including you and me. This is called having an evil nature in our hearts. But, even when people became bad because of sin, God is still good and all-powerful.

God gives people the ability to choose good or bad just like He allowed Adam and Eve to make their bad choice even though He could have stopped them from sinning at any moment. God allows you to make bad decisions too. He will also allow painful results for those bad decisions you make. Very often bad things are happening because people are reaping what they sowed. They might have sowed a small lemon seed and with time will reap a whole lemon tree. God really wants to save people from sin and its consequences; that's why He allows pain into our lives. It's not because He is mean but because He loves us and wants us to turn to Him. Sometimes, the only way God can get our attention is by letting us feel pain and face our need for Him. This is why God doesn't stop all the bad things from happening. God waits and desires that more people may be saved, turn from their wrong ways and come to the knowledge of the truth. Even to this day, many people still haven't come to God, and when everything seems good in their life, they appear to have no need for God. The truth is everyone needs God. He cares and has compassion toward all people who suffer. He has the power to stop all the wrong things at any time, and one day He will.

New word: Disobey – to refuse to do what you are told to do (rules, a command, or someone in authority).

Questions to ask:
1. Why are many things not right today, and why are people often not happy?
2. Why did sin come into the world?
3. Do bad things happen to good people?
4. Why doesn't God stop bad things from happening right now?

Read and discuss
Genesis 3:1-19
(The fall of man).

Let's ask God to forgive us because we often disobey Him too.
Dear God, help us with the sin that is in our hearts. I want to love You and obey the good things You command. Let others come to You too. Amen.

11

A SINNER

"But your iniquities have separated you from your God;
And your sins have hidden His face from you, so that He will not hear."
Isaiah 59:2

Sin is when you do what God tells you not to do, like when God tells you to tell the truth, but you lie instead. When you do not do what He wants you to do, that is a sin as well. If you found your neighbor's toy, and don't return it back to them, that's a sin. So, a sin is doing something bad or not doing something good.

God doesn't want anyone to be a bad person. God hates bad things people do; He hates sin. Sin spoiled God's beautiful world and people. When Adam and Eve disobeyed God, they died spiritually; they were separated from God. Their bodies did not die right away. They lived many more years, but they became afraid and ashamed. They felt pain. Doing things your way and not God's way is sinning against the God who made you. Sin breaks your fellowship with God, and you feel distant from Him. Sin makes you unholy, and it keeps you away from God because God is very holy, pure and good.

We are all spiritually separated from God the day we are born. Everyone is a sinner from the day they are born. Sin starts in our hearts, and it begins to control us, forcing us to obey its bad desire. Having fun is not a sin, but you need to make sure what you do is pleasing to God and does not hurt anyone. Sin makes us think that we are better than others. It makes us want the wrong type of fun that doesn't please God and hurts us and others. Sin also, makes us want more and more things just for ourselves. Instead, God wants us to be thankful for what we have, knowing that all the things on earth will not be here forever — only our spirit will live forever.

New word: Separate – cause to move away or be apart.

Questions to ask:
1. What happened to Adam and Eve when they disobeyed God?
2. Who do you sin against when you do things your way instead of God's way?
3. From what day do we become spiritually separated from God?

Read and discuss
Genesis 3:21-24 (God sent men out of the garden of Eden).

Life is terrible without God. Let's ask God to help you love Him so much that you do not want to sin.
Dear God, help us love You more than anything else in this world. Help us want to do what is good. Amen.

12

THE LAW

"Therefore the law is holy,
and the commandment holy and just and good."
Romans 7:12

God created you, and you belong to God. That is why you should live for Him - the way He wants you to live. But how can you know the way God wants you to live? A long time ago, God gave His law to Israelites. He wrote ten rules on a stone, so Israelites could read them and follow them. They are called the Ten Commandments. They teach the right way to think and live, what you can do, and what you shouldn't do. There is no better way to live than the way God teaches through His great law. If you live His way, you will have real joy in life. All of God's law is that you love God more than anybody and anything else and that you love your neighbor. You need to obey God before you obey anybody else.

These perfect laws were given to His people so that all may be well with them. Now, Israelites knew what God expected of them. But, the problem was that no one could follow the rules perfectly. They continued to disobey and sin against God.

Bible says that this whole world is under the influence of Satan, our enemy. Satan cannot create anything, but when God allows Satan can twist good things into bad things. The weather is not bad but Satan once used the weather to kill Job's family. Computers and money are not bad, but the enemy tries to make people use them for the wrong reasons. He will also try to steal your faith, your joy and your desire to serve God. So, don't become too comfortable here on earth where the enemy tries to trick you. Make sure you are always following and humbly submitting to God. You can trust God even when you don't get the answer you are looking for and when those who are doing bad things seem to get away with it. One day, He will get rid of all evil, bring justice to all things, and make things right.

New word: Submit – to accept, obey or follow someone's leading.

Questions to ask:
1. Is God's law holy, just and good?
2. What is God's law for our lives?
3. Why did God give His people laws?

Read and discuss
Exodus 19:16-20; 20:1-21 (God gives the Ten Commandments to Israelites on Mount Sinai).

Let's pray and ask God to help you do right every day in your work and in your play.
Dear God, help us to keep Your law because we want to live for You. May we trust You because You know what's best for us. Amen.

13

THE WAGES OF SIN IS ETERNAL DEATH

"For the wages of sin is death,
but the gift of God is eternal life in Christ Jesus our Lord."
Romans 6:23

The roads we drive on have rules. On some streets we are allowed to drive fast, while on others we need to drive slowly. Drivers who break this law and drive over the speed limit get punished by a police officer. Parents also have rules for their children, and when children choose to disobey a rule, sometimes parents will discipline their children with a punishment to show that what the child did is wrong and not acceptable. Punishment helps a person remember what not to do and helps them to change their bad behavior. Because a punishment doesn't feel good, that person will try not to repeat the wrong.

There are many different laws people make, and when those laws are broken there is a price to be paid. Because God is very holy and always fair, He cannot let anyone do wrong unnoticed. Sin is the breaking of God's law and unrepentant sin also has a price to be paid for.

God does not always punish right away. Sometimes, He waits a long time for us to turn back to Him, so He can forgive us, and so that we can obey Him again. God is very patient, loving and kind to everyone. It hurts God when He sees sin because He knows what horrible things sin does to you and to others. He tells us what to do to be saved and how to avoid the terrible punishment that will come on all disobedient people when they come before God.

"If you endure chastening, God deals with you as with sons; for what son is there whom a father does not chasten? But if you are without chastening, of which all have become partakers, then you are illegitimate and not sons. Furthermore, we have had human fathers who correct us, and we paid them respect. Shall we not much more readily be in subjection to the Father of spirits and live? For they indeed for a few days chastened us as seemed best to them, but He for our profit, that we may be partakers of His holiness. Now no chastening seems to be joyful for the present, but painful; nevertheless, afterward it yields the peaceable fruit of righteousness to those who have been trained by it." Hebrews 12:7-11

New word: Punishment – the price or bad result for an offense.

Questions to ask:
1. How does a punishment help a person change their behavior?
2. Does sin have a price to be paid for?
3. Does God always punish sin right away?

Read and discuss
Genesis 6:5-22 (Noah and the flood).

Let's pray that God would forgive us when we disobey Him and help us follow Him.
Dear God, we know our hearts are very sinful. Even though we deserve to be punished like the wicked people in Noah's day, please be patient and merciful and forgive us for our sins. Give us a clean heart. Help us be obedient. Amen.

14

GOD TAKES CARE OF US

*"For He shall give His angels charge over you,
to keep you in all your ways."
Psalm 91:11*

God loves you very much and will take care of you no matter what happens. Every day and all night, He watches over you. God never sleeps. Long ago, before God made Adam and Eve, He made many angels. They exist to serve and praise God, and they do anything God asks them to do. Angels do many wonderful things, like watch over people or deliver messages to them from God.

When God's children get sick or face sorrow and pain, does that mean God has forgotten to take care of them? No. Some troubles come for our good. The Bible tells a wonderful story about a boy named Joseph. Joseph had many difficulties in his life, but God used all of Joseph's problems for his good and for the good of God's people by saving them from a strong famine.

God deeply cares about everything that happens. You can talk to God about all the little things in your life not just the "big stuff." God wants to do good things in your life more than you can ever imagine!

New word: Watch – keep under careful or protective observation.

Questions to ask:
1. When does God watch over you?
2. Can God use troubles for your good?
3. What kind of things can you talk to God about?

Read and discuss
Daniel 6:16-23 (Daniel in the lion's den),
Genesis 45:1-8 (Joseph revealed to his brothers).

Let's pray and thank God for His great care for you.

Dear God, thank You for giving me food, water, clothes and many other good things.
I know that all things work together for good for those that love God. Amen.

15

JESUS CAME FROM HEAVEN

*"For you know the grace of our Lord Jesus Christ,
that though He was rich, yet for your sakes He became poor,
that you through His poverty might become rich."
2 Corinthians 8:9*

Jesus, the Son of God, lived in heaven with God the Father and God the Holy Spirit long before the earth was made. After sin came into the world, God felt sorry about the sorrow and trouble that began because of sin. And God said, "This world needs a Savior." So, God the Son decided to enter our world as a man called Jesus.

Jesus was born as a tiny baby; He became just like us except that He had no sin. What a change it was for Jesus to come down from heaven to earth! He was rich in heaven; everything was His. When He came down to earth, He became poor. He left it all to become your Savior! Jesus left His beautiful home and comfort in heaven, His Father, angels, security, and praise.

Jesus grew up and lived a perfect life doing many good things. On earth, Jesus had a big family; He had younger brothers and sisters. As the oldest son, Jesus spent most of His life ministering to His family and preparing for His ministry. He was very good and kind. When He was about 33 years old, some people who hated Him nailed Him to a wooden cross to die. But, Jesus knew the real reason why He was going to die. He knew that He came down from heaven to our sinful earth to take the punishment for the sins of the whole world and become our Savior! All the wrong that we have done was paid for by Jesus. Oh, how good God is! How He loves you!

Why would Jesus want to take our punishment on Himself? Because He loves us so much! Jesus wanted to pay the price for us to have a restored friendship with our Father in Heaven and to give us new hearts. Everyone sins even grown-ups, and sin must be punished. Sin puts fun, play and other things first above God. But, God loves us so much that He paid for our punishment through His Son Jesus on the cross. If you believe in Jesus, your sins will be forgiven, and you will live with Him forever. Only Jesus can save people from their sins.

New word: Savior – someone who saves you from danger.

Questions to ask:
1. Where did Jesus live before He came to earth?
2. Who did Jesus become like when He came to earth?
3. Why did Jesus come down to earth?

Read and discuss
John 3:16-17 (God sent His Son into the world),
Luke 2:1-20 (Jesus's birth).

Let's pray and thank God for His great gift of salvation.
Dear God, thank You for loving us so much and sending Your Son down to be born on this earth to teach us and save us from our sin. Jesus, thank You for leaving Your home in heaven to be my hero. Amen.

16

JESUS OBEYED GOD

"And being found in appearance as a man,
He humbled himself,
and became obedient to the point of death,
even the death of the cross."
Philippians 2:8

When Jesus came to earth, Satan tried to make Jesus disobey God just like he tempted Adam and Eve in the garden to sin against God. But, Jesus loved God the Father very much, and He obeyed God. Every day, from morning till night, Jesus always obeyed God. He always did the will of God the Father and never did anything wrong.

Jesus was fully man and fully God when He walked on earth. This is hard for us to understand or explain, but that's what the Bible tells us. Jesus had the supernatural power to forgive sin and raise the dead, but Jesus was also born as a human being with a physical body. That means there were times Jesus felt tired, hungry, in pain, and tempted. He also prayed and had to learn things just as we do.

Although Jesus had the power of God to do anything He wanted at any time, He chose to limit Himself to our human level to be on our level! At times you might want to play outside a little more but you listen to your parents when they ask you to come inside. Sometimes, parents limit themselves too. They'll sit on the floor to play with a crawling baby; instead of driving a nice small car, they get a minivan for their children's comfort; or they like to sleep in on Saturday morning, but instead they'll attend to their children's need early in the morning. What a great example of obedience and humility Jesus left for us. You can be sure that Jesus understands everything about you and everything you go through because He went through it too.

New word: Humble – not showing or not considering yourself or your ideas to be as important.

Questions to ask:
1. Did Jesus always obey God?
2. Was Jesus fully God as He walked on earth?
3. Was Jesus fully man as He walked on earth?

Read and discuss
Matthew 4:1-11 (Jesus is tempted by Satan).

Let's thank Jesus for being so humble and obedient to His Father.
Dear Jesus, thank You for being an example for me. Thank You for obeying God even when it was hard and caused You pain. Help me when I feel tempted to do something wrong. You know what it feels like to live on this earth. Help me obey God's will every day. Amen.

17

JESUS TAUGHT PEOPLE

*"But Simon Peter answered Him, "Lord, to whom shall we go?
You have the words of eternal life."
John 6:68*

Everywhere Jesus went He would teach others. Sometimes, Jesus sat in a boat at the lake teaching people that stood on the shore. At times, He stood on the porch of the Temple and talked to people. He taught people as He walked through the streets or sat on a hill.

Jesus did not teach people how to read and write. He taught something more important than that. He taught the most important thing in the whole world — knowledge of God. He told people about God's love. He helped them see how terrible the sin is that is deep down in their hearts. He told them that He came to die for their sin, so they could be God's children. He also warned about the punishment that would come to all who do not listen to God's commands.

All kinds of people liked to listen to Jesus. Rich, poor, young, old, and people from many countries would listen to His teachings. The little children wanted to hear Him too. Some grown-ups don't like to spend time with kids, but Jesus loved children! Jesus was the best teacher. He taught others by showing an example, by asking questions and telling interesting stories called parables. At times, He repeated himself if it was important. He also made powerful statements that were easy to remember. Jesus was a very wise teacher.

New word: Parable – a simple story that teaches a moral or spiritual lesson.

Questions to ask:
1. Where did Jesus teach others?
2. Who liked to listen to Jesus?
3. What are some of the things Jesus used to teach others?

Read and discuss
Matthew 5:1-12 (The Beatitudes).

Let's thank Jesus for being a wonderful teacher.
Dear Jesus, thank You for the instructive stories You told to help me remember Your lessons. Help me keep Your words in my heart, so I will always think about what's right and about Your love for me. Amen.

18

JESUS RULES OVER SICKNESS AND DEATH. HE FORGIVES SIN

"Then fear came upon all, and they glorified God, saying,
"A great prophet has risen up among us"; and,
"God has visited His people.""
Luke 7:16

Jesus said that He was the Son of God and that He came from God. He showed that He came from God by doing many wonderful works. He calmed the stormy wind and the sea; He healed every kind of sickness; and He could even make people who died come back to life! Even today God can heal our sickness when we pray in the name of Jesus. He has the power to make us better if that is His will.

Since Jesus is God, He can forgive our sins. If you tell Him you are sorry and ask Him to forgive you, He will forgive all of your sins. It is never too late to ask for forgiveness, no matter how big your sin might feel. God is always willing to forgive and forget your sin and give you a fresh start.

Forgiving your sins is much more important than healing a physical sickness. That's because we will have new, healthy bodies in heaven. But, we can only enter heaven when Jesus takes away our sins. When Jesus forgives our sins, we can have a close and personal relationship with Him for the rest of our lives and even after we die. We'll be with Him in paradise forever. Getting to know Jesus will take time, like with any other relationship, so the more you spend time with Him, the more you will get to know Him. With time, you will start to enjoy and appreciate Jesus more and more. Jesus desires to be your closest friend, and He alone is your Lord! He is both your friend and your God.

New word: Lord – someone who has power, authority, and influence; a master or ruler.

Questions to ask:
1. How did Jesus show that He came from God?
2. Is it too late to ask Jesus for forgiveness of sins?
3. Is Jesus both your friend and your God?

Read and discuss

Luke 8:40-56 (A girl restored to life, and a woman healed),
Mark 2:1-12 (Jesus forgives and heals a paralytic).

Let's thank God for sending Jesus and for many wonderful miracles that Jesus did when He was on this earth.

Dear God, thank You for all of the wonderful miracles that Jesus did for people while He lived here on earth. Thank You for healing my heart when You forgave my sins. I want to have a close friendship with You for my whole life, and I'm happy to know I can see You in heaven one day. Amen.

19

JESUS DIED FOR YOU

"Therefore My Father loves Me,
because I lay down My life that I may take it again.
No one takes it from Me, but I lay it down of Myself.
I have power to lay it down, and I have power to take it again.
This command I have received from My Father."
John 10:17-18

Wherever Jesus went He was always doing good, but some people hated Him because they were jealous of His popularity and hated His teachings. Satan is God's greatest enemy and tries to make people hate God as well. One day, these people who hated Jesus took Him to Pontius Pilate who was the Roman governor in Judea. They lied by telling Pilate that Jesus is a bad man who was making trouble and that they should get rid of Him. Pilate asked, "What bad things has He done?" Nobody could think of even one bad thing Jesus had done. But they said, "He ought to die anyway. You must crucify him!" Because Pilate was afraid of the people, he said, "You take Him and put Him to death by nailing Him to a cross." And that is what they did. Jesus was terribly beaten and made fun of. He was forced to carry the cross up a hill called Golgotha, and then they nailed His hands and feet to the wooden cross.

Those men did not take away Jesus's life; Jesus actually chose to lay it down Himself. He came to earth for that reason: to carry the heavy load of punishment for your sins! Even before Jesus gave His life away on the cross, He gave His life to others by serving them daily. What a great love He has for people! Even as Jesus hung on that cross, He prayed for His enemies. He wanted them to be saved! The Son of God died on a cross like a criminal because He loves you.

New word: Governor – the person in authority, who is appointed to govern a town or region.

Questions to ask:
1. Did anyone hate Jesus?
2. To whom was Jesus taken by the people who hated Him?
3. Did men take Jesus's life from Him?

Read and discuss
John 19:1-20 (Pilate's decision. The King on a cross).

Let's thank Jesus for dying on the cross for us.
Dear Jesus, I can never thank You enough for dying on the cross for me. You loved me so much that You gave up Your life to pay for my punishment. I want to love You by giving You my life. Amen.

20

JESUS LIVES AGAIN

"He was buried, and He rose again the third day according to the Scriptures."
1 Corinthians 15:4

Those who loved Jesus were very sad when He died. They had expected Him to be their Savior and King on earth, but how could He be their Savior if He was now dead? They did not understand. After Jesus died, He was taken off the cross and buried in a new tomb. A large stone was placed against the door of the tomb, and guards were set to make sure the tomb was protected.

But, Jesus did exactly what He said He would do. He finished the job God had given Him. Jesus Himself told His disciples earlier that He would rise from the dead to live forever once He carried the punishment for all sin. When He arose from the dead, He showed Himself to His disciples and to others many times in His risen body before going up to heaven.

One day, when Jesus was with His disciples, He walked with them to the town of Bethany and led them up on a hill called Mount of Olives. There, He talked to His disciples face to face for the last time. When He had finished speaking, He lifted His hands to bless them. While He blessed them, Jesus began to go up and up until a cloud came and hid Him. Jesus ascended, He is alive now – He is the Son of God. Jesus is in heaven now in His risen body.

New word: Ascended – the going up of Jesus into heaven on the fortieth day after the Resurrection.

Questions to ask:
1. What did Jesus do once He rose from the dead?
2. What happened on Mount of Olives when Jesus was blessing His disciples?
3. Where is Jesus now?

Read and discuss

Matthew 28:1-8 (Jesus has risen),
John 20:19-31 (Jesus came in the midst of His disciples),
Luke 24:50-53 (The Ascension).

Let's thank God that Jesus was able to complete the task that God had given Him to do.
Dear God, thank You for Your perfect son Jesus that You sent to teach us and die for us. Thank You that He has paid for my sin. Thank You that He still watches over me. Amen.

21

JESUS PRAYS FOR YOU

"Therefore He is also able to save to the uttermost
those who come to God through Him,
since He always lives to make intercession for them."
Hebrews 7:25

Jesus is God and knows every one of your weaknesses and all of your strengths. He knows what struggles you are facing today. He knows everything that will happen in your life, and even before it happens, Jesus has already prayed for it!

Jesus speaks to God in your defense. He is faithful even when you are not faithful to Him! Parents aren't perfect, but they still love their children even if the kids are being disobedient. Imagine how much more a perfect God is trustworthy to love you even when you disobey Him.

You need help to live for God. Even if you have a new heart, seeds of sin still try to grow. Just like in a garden, you can pull out all the weeds today, but tomorrow new weeds are growing again. It is so good to know that Jesus prays for you to His Father, and you can also pray to Him for help.

Jesus told His disciples that God will give us every good thing we ask for. If you ask Him, He will surely help you be good. God will never tell you, "Don't bother me." He knows it is hard for you to live for Him the way you should. He knows that you are weak and have sinful desires, and He is glad to help you pull the weeds of sin out of your heart. You should tell God what those weeds are and ask Him to make you want to pull them out. Ask Him to make you strong, to do what is right, and to say "no" to all that is wrong.

New word: Intercession – to come between so as to stop or change a result on behalf of another.

Questions to ask:
1. Who does Jesus pray to God for?
2. Is Jesus faithful even when you are not faithful to Him?
3. Can seeds of sin still try to grow in a new heart?

Read and discuss
Luke 22:31-32
(Jesus tells Peter that He prayed for him),
John 17:1-26
(Jesus prays for His disciples
and for all believers).

Let's thank God for His Son Jesus who is alive to pray for you!

Dear God, thank You for Your Son Jesus who prays perfect prayers for me! Thank You that He prays for my heart to love and trust You. Help me when seeds of sin try to grow in my heart. Amen.

22

THE HOLY SPIRIT

"On the last day, that great day of the feast, Jesus stood and cried out,
saying, "If anyone thirsts, let him come to Me and drink.
He who believes in Me, as the Scripture has said,
out of his heart will flow rivers of living water."
But this He spoke concerning the Spirit, whom those believing in Him
would receive; for the Holy Spirit was not yet given,
because Jesus was not yet glorified."
John 7:37-39

The Holy Spirit is God. Holy Spirit has been working from the very beginning when the world was being created. Other names for the Holy Spirit are the Spirit of Jesus, Helper, Comforter, and the Spirit of Truth. After Jesus rose from the dead, He spent 40 days with His disciples. He told them about many things and about the Spirit whom the Heavenly Father would send to them.

The Holy Spirit came down on the disciples to be with them and to live in them on a special day called the Pentecost. Before the Pentecost, when there was an important job to be done, God chose a person to do it, and the Holy Spirit gave that person power and ability to get the job done. In the Bible, you can read about a man called Bezalel who received special artistic abilities from the Holy Spirit to make a beautiful temple for God. Holy Spirit gave David the power to rule a nation. Jephthah received military skill. Samson got supernatural strength. Zechariah was given a word of prophecy, and there were others upon whom the Spirit came to give them special abilities for their job. No one can control the work of the Holy Spirit. He works in different ways, but He will never go against God's character or God's Word. His work in a person's life can be named the most powerful work in this world! Holy Spirit helps a person know his or her sin and come to God in repentance. Repentance is when you feel regret for the things you've done wrong, and you turn away from doing those things. Holy Spirit also puts faith in your heart as you hear from the Word of God. He helps you believe that Jesus is the only way back to the Father in heaven and makes you become born into God's family. When you hear the Word of God, it is the Spirit who makes you spiritually alive. Eternal life comes through the Spirit. Where the Spirit of the Lord is there is freedom from sin and condemnation!

New word: Faith – a strong belief, complete trust or confidence in someone or something.

Questions to ask:
1. Has God the Holy Spirit been working from the very beginning?
2. What's the name of the day when the Holy Spirit came down on disciples?
3. Is it true that the Holy Spirit works in different ways? Will He ever go against God's character or God's Word?

Read and discuss
Judges 3:7-11 (The Spirit of the Lord came upon Othniel),
Acts 2:1-18 (Coming of the Holy Spirit).

Let's thank God for sending us the Holy Spirit.
Dear God, thank You for sending down Your Holy Spirit into this world. Thank You for showing us our sins and helping our hearts come to You for forgiveness. Let me receive this powerful Holy Spirit that Jesus had upon Him. And, please help more people in every part of the world turn away from their sin and believe in Your Son Jesus. Let them be born again so they can join our big, heavenly family. Amen.

23

THE WORK OF THE HOLY SPIRIT

"And these signs will follow those who believe:
in My name they will cast out demons;
they will speak with new tongues; they will take up serpents,
and if they drink anything deadly, it will by no means hurt them;
they will lay hands on the sick, and they will recover."
Mark 16:17-18

You cannot see the Holy Spirit, but He is real and powerful. You can see the works He is doing in your life and in the lives of other believers. We can see the change in the lives of Jesus's disciples. The night when the soldiers came to take Jesus, His disciples ran away because they were afraid for their lives. After Jesus rose from the dead, He told His disciples to go and tell everyone about Him. But, how could they? They weren't brave enough. Disciples needed the power of the Holy Spirit to accomplish this mission. Holy Spirit came down on the disciples and filled them with courage they never had before. That's what the Spirit does. He gives you the power to live a holy life and guides you into doing God's will. He does this by making you want to be more like Christ; helping you become more like Him; teaching you all things; reminding you of Jesus's words; and giving you the power and ability to share about Jesus with others. Even when you don't know the right words to pray, the Holy Spirit prays with you and for you. He gives you deep peace, comforts and guides you into truth. He even gives insight into God's thoughts, His plans, and the future! No one knows the thoughts of God except the Spirit of God.

Once the disciples received the Holy Spirit, they risked everything to spread the news about Jesus. Many of them were rejected, beaten, put in prisons and killed. They risked their lives for something they knew was true: Jesus was raised from the dead, and they had received the power of the Holy Spirit! God has important work for you to do too, and you can only do it by the power of the Holy Spirit.

New word: Power – the ability to do something or act in a particular way.

Questions to ask:
1. Can you see the Holy Spirit?
2. Did the lives of Jesus's disciples change once they received the Holy Spirit?
3. How does the Holy Spirit help you live a holy life and do God's will?

Read and discuss
Acts 5:17-32 (Apostles imprisoned).

Let's thank God for the Holy Spirit who helps you deal with problems.

Dear God, thank You for Your Holy Spirit who helps me obey You and gives me courage to tell others about Jesus. Please send me your Holy Spirit to live in my heart forever. Amen.

24

THE GIFTS AND THE FRUIT OF THE SPIRIT

"But the fruit of the Spirit is love, joy, peace, longsuffering, kindness, goodness, faithfulness, gentleness, self-control.
Against such there is no law."
Galatians 5:22-23

The fruit of the Spirit is the result of the Holy Spirit working in you. To have the fruit of the Spirit, you need to abide in Jesus. Throughout your life, as you get filled with the Holy Spirit, you will notice your character change. You will grow in love and kindness toward others, and you will feel peace and joy. When things happen that make you upset, you will not be as angry as you used to be. You will also have the power to tell others about God. That doesn't mean that you will always feel powerful. Often, it is when you feel the weakest but stay obedient to God that the Lord does His greatest work through you. So, don't wait to feel powerful; reach out to meet the needs of others.

The spiritual gifts are special abilities given to a person by the Holy Spirit. They are abilities given so we can minister to the needs of other believers. There are many gifts, and some people have more than one gift. You are responsible for the way you use your gifts.

Did you know that you can grieve the Holy Spirit? When you are not kind to others, don't forgive, desire to do wrong, become extremely angry, yell, or tell lies, this grieves the Holy Spirit who lives inside you. Your body is a temple of the Holy Spirit. You need to make sure your body is clean from sin because it also belongs to God.

New word: Abide – to continue in something.

Questions to ask:
1. What do you need to do to have the fruit of the Spirit like joy, love, peace, and kindness?
2. Are spiritual gifts special abilities that are given to a person by the Holy Spirit?
3. Can you grieve the Holy Spirit?

Read and discuss
1 Corinthians 12:4-11 (Spiritual gifts).

Let's thank God for His Spirit who gives us good fruit and special gifts.
Dear God, thank You for making my character more loving. Please produce good fruit in my life. Show me the special gifts Your Spirit has given me and how I can use these gifts to serve others. Help me to never grieve the Holy Spirit. Amen.

BEING FILLED WITH THE HOLY SPIRIT

"And do not be drunk with wine, in which is dissipation;
but be filled with the Spirit, speak to one another in psalms
and hymns and spiritual songs, singing and making melody
in your heart to the Lord, giving thanks always for all things
to God the Father in the name of our Lord Jesus Christ,
submitting to one another in the fear of God."
Ephesians 5:18-21

You are like a container that is meant to be filled with something. There are many important things that you can fill your life with like work, family, church activities, hobbies, and other things. All of these things can make you very busy but still leave your life feeling empty. That is because you are made to be filled with God's presence. Your soul thirsts for God! Every Christian needs daily filling of the Holy Spirit to live the Christian life.

Sometimes, great Spirit-filled believers like apostle Paul, King David, and even Jesus felt frustrations, discouragements and disappointments. Being Spirit-filled will not always make you feel happy, but it will help you handle disappointments in a different way. It will not make all of your problems disappear, but it will give you strength and wisdom to deal with them better. Some people who are Spirit-filled may actually experience more temptation than those who are not. Jesus was filled with the Holy Spirit, but He was tempted by Satan in the desert.

To be filled with the Holy Spirit, you need to be cleansed from every known sin in your life. Don't make excuses by saying, "It's just been a bad day." This will keep the Holy Spirit from filling you up with his presence. Every area of your life needs to be submitted to God, not just the spiritual part. Your play, your school, your work, and your plans should be given to God. As you begin your Christian life in the Spirit, you should walk and grow with the Spirit. When you listen to the Holy Spirit and do what He tells you to do, you will bear the good fruit and have a more Christ-like character.

New word: Filled – put something into a container so that it is completely full; to become full of something.

Questions to ask:
1. What are you made to be filled with?
2. Does every Christian need a daily filling of the Holy Spirit?
3. Should every area of your life be submitted to God or just the spiritual part?

Read and discuss
Acts 5:1-16 (Ananias and Sapphira lie to God and His people).

Let's thank God that He fills us with His wonderful Spirit.

Dear God, thank You for giving me Your Spirit. Please fill me up with Your presence daily and cleanse me from all of my sins. Please help me be honest about my sin and not let it grow in my heart. Heal me from the hurt that sin has caused in my heart. Amen.

26

BECOMING CHILD OF GOD

"If we confess our sins,
He is faithful and just to forgive us our sins
and to cleanse us from all unrighteousness."
1 John 1:9

God is holy. He cannot allow what is evil to continue forever. God cannot ignore sin. He is not like us – He is perfect. He is righteous and just in all His actions. He never makes a mistake. We as people are the very opposite of God; we have become bad, and we want to do bad things. Yet, the holy God loves us and wants us to become His children. God welcomes you into His family! That is why He sent His Son to earth to take the right punishment for your sins by dying on the cross. God knew people would turn away from Him, so He had a plan to send Jesus Christ to become our only way of escape from eternal death. Now through Jesus, God will not turn you away if you believe in His Son. Come to Him and ask Him to forgive you of your sins. He will forgive you and save you from eternal death. "He who believes in the Son has everlasting life; and he who does not believe the Son shall not see life, but the wrath of God abides on him." John 3:36 There is no other way; you cannot save yourself no matter how hard you want to or try. No one can! Without Jesus, we would all perish. God knew we couldn't do it by ourselves, so He created this way to save us. It was God who reached down to us first. It was His idea to save us. The Bible tells us that Christ was chosen to die for our sins even before the world began! An angel appeared to Joseph in a dream and said that "Mary will bring forth a Son, and you shall call His name Jesus for He will save His people from their sins (Mathew 1:20-21)." He has already done His part. Now it is your turn to make a choice and invite Jesus to be the Lord of your life. There is joy in the presence of the angles of God over one sinner who repents! Like a woman who has found her lost coin and calls her friends and neighbors to rejoice with her, for she has found the coin which she had lost!

New word: Eternal – lasting or continuing forever, with no beginning or end.

Questions to ask:

1. Does the holy God want you to become His child?
2. Is there any way you can save yourself from eternal death other than through Jesus?
3. Did people reach out to God first?

Read and discuss

Luke 15:1-10 (The parable of the lost sheep and coin).

Let's come to God in prayer just as you are, with your sinful heart and pray the most important prayer together.

Dear Heavenly Father, I admit that I am a sinner. I thank You that Jesus died instead of me for my sins. I ask You to forgive me of my sins. I trust in Jesus as the Lord of my life. Father, I trust You to give me the gift of salvation. Amen.

27

SALVATION

"He has delivered us from the power of darkness and conveyed us into the kingdom of the Son of His love, in whom we have redemption through His blood, the forgiveness of sins."
Colossians 1:13-14

Salvation is God's gift to you. You cannot buy it, earn it, or deserve it in any way. Your best efforts cannot come anywhere close to paying the price for salvation. Only Jesus's sacrifice on the cross achieved God's requirement for our forgiveness of sins.

You receive salvation only when you believe in Jesus Christ and acknowledge your sins. That's when God forgives you of all of your sins and says you are not guilty of them anymore. God canceled the punishment that should have been yours. God wipes out your bad record and applies Jesus's clean record to you! This fixes your relationship with God, and you become a child of God. Jesus bought you with his life. You don't need to be afraid of death or punishment anymore because He gives you eternal life. He gave you a new and good heart — a heart that loves God and a heart that wants to please God.

New word: Salvation – something that saves from danger, loss, or failure.

Questions to ask:
1. Is salvation a gift from God?
2. Can you buy it, earn it, or deserve it in any way?
3. How can anyone receive salvation?

Read and discuss
John 3:1-5 (Nicodemus; the new birth).

Let's thank God for your forgiveness, and that this forgiveness is not based on how we feel or what we can accomplish but on God's promise to us.

Dear God, thank You for saving me from the punishment of my sins. Thank You for Jesus who had to feel all of the pain that I deserved. Jesus, thank You for loving me so much that You gave Your life for me! Remind me that I am forgiven by Your grace. Remind me that I don't ever have to earn Your love but that You give it to me freely. You are such a good God! Amen.

28

NEW CREATION

*"Therefore, if anyone is in Christ, he is a new creation;
old things have passed away; behold, all things have become new."*
2 Corinthians 5:17

Your eternal life began the moment you trusted Jesus with your salvation! Of course, this new life will get a lot better once you are in heaven. But, God is now your Father, and you are His child. Nothing can separate you from His unchanging love! There is nothing you can do to stop Him from being faithful to His own promise.

You are a "new creation." This doesn't mean that when you look in the mirror, you will see a different face. Your home and toys stay the same, but on the inside, you will try to act more and more like Jesus. If you really are God's child, you will love Him more and more. You will want to give Him the very best that you have. You will also love others because your Heavenly Father loves them. A desire to pray and read God's Word will fill your heart. There are many good books to read, but the Bible is the most important book in the world.

God is the great Giver — everything you have He has given to you! You become more like Him when you give to the poor or when you give to help missionaries do their job. You can also say kind words and do kind things to people all around you. Jesus says that when you give something to someone else because of your love for Jesus, then it's like you are really giving it to him! Isn't that wonderful? Дарить

New word: Unchanging Love – love that remains the same, it does not change.

Questions to ask:
1. When does your eternal life begin?
2. Can anything separate you from God's love?
3. How can you be more like God who is the great Giver?

Read and discuss
John 12:1-3 (Mary's gift to Jesus).

Let's thank God for His unchanging love and for making you a new creation.

Dear God, thank You for changing me on the inside. Thank You for making me Your child and welcoming me into Your family. Thank You for making my dead spirit alive again! You are a great Giver, and I want to serve You by giving to others. Amen.

29

NEW LIFE

*"For by one offering He has perfected forever
those who are being sanctified."*
Hebrews 10:14

At the moment of your salvation God changed your spiritual person. God has already made you holy, and He is continuing to making you holy. Now you don't have to try really hard to become something that you are not. Instead, you are only beginning to live out who you already are. You can't enjoy bad things the same way you used to. For a moment it might seem fun to do something bad, like taking something that doesn't belong to you or not telling the truth, but you will only be left feeling sad. You cannot be ok with sin in your life because that would mean that you don't care about the heart and the desires of your Heavenly Father.

Often, you have a choice to do good or to do bad, and sometimes it's a really hard choice to make. You need to remember that your Heavenly Father has given you the strength to make the right decisions. And, you can ask Jesus to help you. Jesus lives in you now, and He is stronger than any sin. That means sin doesn't have the power over you that it had in the past.

You can give all of your money to God, but if you really love Him, you will obey Him. To obey is more important than to give. Obedience is the most important way to show God that you love Him.

New word: Sanctify – to set apart and to make holy.

Questions to ask:
1. Are you already made holy and will you continue to be made holy?
2. Do you have the strength to make the right choice?
3. What is even more important than giving?

Read and discuss
Daniel 3:8-30 (Saved in the fiery trial).

Let's thank God for changing you into a good person and helping you obey Him with your heart.

Dear God, thank You for the new life that You have given me. Teach me to obey You with my heart and not just look like I'm obeying You on the outside. Remind me to come to You and ask for forgiveness and strength when I sin against You. Remind me that even on those bad days, You will not love me any less than You already do right now. Amen.

30

SPIRITUAL GROWTH

"being confident of this very thing,
that He who has begun a good work in you will complete it."
Philippians 1:6

You need to grow spiritually and it takes time; there are no shortcuts. It's your daily desires, choices and actions that will affect your growth. When you do something repeatedly, it affects the direction your life will take. Attending church, reading the Bible, and praying can help you grow spiritually but only if you do these things because of your faith in Christ.

You cannot create your own spiritual growth; that is God's job. Even God's law cannot make you grow; it can only show you the direction in which God is going to grow you. But, you can be obedient with the way God grows you. He wants to see you grow, and He is committed to growing you. God wants to grow your love and knowledge of Him. He wants to strengthen your relationship with Him. He is like a very caring gardener who takes good care of his garden. He plants, waters and trims the plants to keep them healthy.

When you sin, it harms you and those around you, and your Heavenly Father will lovingly correct and discipline you. Even when you are dealing with problems in your life, God is growing you! And, that should make you happy. Not happy about the problem, but about the good that God is doing in your life through those problems. You can easily see physical growth happening from the outside, but spiritual growth begins from the inside, with your mind and heart. Sometimes, you might want to lie because you don't want to face the consequences for what you did. But, when you think about what God wants — that He doesn't want you to lie — you are able to say the truth. Instead of thinking, "This lie will make my life better," you'll think, "This lie will hurt God's heart." Having the right mindset will help you make the right choice! In Revelation 22:15, it is written that whoever loves and practices a lie will not enter through the gates into the heavenly city.

New word: Growth – the process of increasing or developing in size, quality, or amount.
Questions to ask:
1. Does growing spiritually take time?
2. Can you create your own growth?
3. Does God want to see you grow? Is He committed to growing you spiritually?

Read and discuss
John 15:1-8 (The true vine).

Let's pray and ask God to help you to trust Him and to be patient as you become more and more like Jesus.

Dear God, please continue to grow my heart and mind to be like Jesus. You are like a good gardener, and I am like a plant that You love to take care of. Let me become beautiful, strong and full of spiritual fruit. Amen.

TELLING OTHERS ABOUT JESUS

"Go therefore and make disciples of all the nations,
baptizing them in the name of the Father and of the Son
and of the Holy Spirit, teaching them to observe all things
that I have commanded you; and lo, I am with you always,
even to the end of the age."
Matthew 28:19-20

Have you heard about David, the shepherd boy? He made sweet music with his harp and made up many songs about God. David was continually thinking about God. Therefore, he grew up to be a great man of God. We too can think about God every day at all times! When you think of Him while you work and play, you will try to please Him. This will help you grow up to be a strong man and woman of God, and you will have many things to share with others about Jesus, bringing them to the Kingdom of Heaven too. God commands us and helps us to share the Good News about Jesus with others. Many people still have not heard about Jesus and His wonderful love for us. Satan, God's enemy, does not want you to tell others about God's love. He will try to make you feel scared or think that you have nothing to share, but you can always tell the story of how you came to trust Jesus. Very often, when you live your life for Jesus, others will notice and will ask you how come you live so differently than other people they know. Those are also great opportunities to share about Jesus.

Sometimes, God's children have to suffer for Jesus's sake. When Jesus was on earth, He told His disciples that they would suffer for Him. Jesus was hated by some people, and often His followers are hated too. God reminds us that any suffering on earth is very short compared to the joy and reward you will have in heaven. Jesus said, "Blessed are you when they revile and persecute you, and say all kinds of evil against you falsely for My sake. Rejoice and be exceedingly glad, for great is your reward in heaven, for so they persecuted the prophets who were before you." Matthew 5:11-12

New word: Disciple – a follower of a leader or teacher.

Questions to ask:
1. Who was David, the great man of God, continually thinking about?
2. Does God command you and help you to share about Jesus with others?
3. Will God's children ever have to suffer because of their faith in Jesus?

Read and discuss
Acts 7:54-60 (Stephen the Martyr).

Let's thank God for the missionaries and preachers who go far away to tell about Jesus even if it brings them suffering.

Dear God, thank You for the men and women who love You so much that they will go to scary and dangerous places to tell others about Your Son Jesus. Please bless their work and fill my thoughts with You, so I can also tell people around me about Your goodness and love. Amen.

32
PRAYER

*"Be anxious for nothing,
but in everything by prayer and supplication, with thanksgiving,
let your requests be made known to God."*
Philippians 4:6

When we pray, we talk to God who listens and answers. While Jesus was on earth, He also prayed to His Father very often. Jesus liked to be alone to talk with His Father. Sometimes, it was early in the mornings or late at night.

God wants you to be open and to ask Him for anything you need or like if you think it is good for you. God wants you to tell Him your troubles and to ask Him for help. He wants you to pray for others, for your family and for missionaries, so more people will come to Jesus. He even wants you to pray for your enemies, for boys and girls who do bad things. Through your prayers, God does His will on earth! You can pray to Him at church with other people or when you are at home with your family. You can pray to Him even when you are alone while you are walking down the street or while you are playing. No matter where you are, you can pray to Him because God is everywhere.

We fold our hands and close our eyes to help us think only about God and what we are saying to Him. But, you can also pray in your heart without closing your eyes or folding your hands.

God can give you what you ask for, but there are many reasons why He doesn't always do that. God always does what is best for His children. He knows even better than your daddy and mommy about what is right for you and what is not good for you. You must learn to trust God. At times, He will say yes, sometimes He will say no, and other times He will tell you to wait.

New word: Supplication – asking or begging for something strongly or humbly.

Questions to ask:
1. Did Jesus pray?
2. Where can you pray to God?
3. Does God always do what is best for His children?

Read and discuss
Matthew 6:5-15 (The model prayer).

Let's take time to ask and thank God for the things He has given us.
Dear God, please provide all that my family needs every day. I trust You with the things I want and with my future. Help anyone who is mean and unloving to change in their hearts. Thank You for hearing me when I pray to You. Teach me to ask You for the things that will please you. Amen.

33

THE BIBLE

*"The grass withers, the flower fades,
but the word of our God stands forever."*
Isaiah 40:8

The Bible was written over a period of 1,500 years. It was written in different places like prisons, lonely islands and palaces. Bible is the only book that was written by God. To write His Word God used different kinds of people like kings, fishermen, farmers and pastors. Yet, you will not find any messages that say the opposite of one another. The whole Bible carries the same message, even on many hard subjects! That's because God is the author.

The entire Bible, not just some of it, was inspired by God. God wrote the books through the hands of over 40 different people. Most of those authors we know, but there are a few anonymous writers too. You can be sure that God is powerful enough to make sure each one of His books is included in the Bible. Bible can be trusted more than your feelings and opinions. Bible can be trusted more than what society says and what anybody's values say, both of which are constantly changing with time. Bible is filled with God's truth telling you how to get from where you are to where you want to be. Bible is your guidebook for life — you should turn to it regularly!

Bible has been translated into many different languages. As of fall 2017, the full Bible has been translated into more than 650 languages. Just the New Testament is translated into over 1,500 languages! The Bible is the final answer to our questions. Many lives have been changed because of the Bible. It is the world's best-selling book and stands above all other books. Bible is always right and should be your final authority. God has chosen to show you what He is like and what He wants you to be like through the Bible. You should listen to your parents, teachers, law enforcement, and doctors, but even more, you should obey the Bible. You should check what other people teach you with what the Bible says. Some people will try to change what the Bible is saying to say something they want. They want to trick you to believe a lie about God. That is why we should be careful and have a personal relationship with God, who is the author of the Bible.

New word: Author – a writer of a book, story, article, report etc.

Questions to ask:
1. How long did it take to write the Bible?
2. Do all messages of the Bible support each other?
3. Is God the author of the entire Bible or just some of it?

Read and discuss
Luke 4:16-21 (Jesus says Scripture is fulfilled).

Let's thank God for creating a perfect Bible through so many imperfect people!

Dear God, thank You for using different people to tells us about who You are through your Word. Thank You for the wisdom and truth You teach us. Thank You for telling us about Your love for us. Help me to love Your Word more and to obey it every day. Amen.

UNDERSTANDING THE BIBLE

"Let the word of Christ dwell in you richly in all wisdom,
teaching and admonishing one another in psalms and hymns
and spiritual songs, singing with grace in your hearts to the Lord."
Colossians 3:16

Understanding the Bible doesn't always happen quickly; it takes thinking, prayer and time. We need to love the Bible deeply. When you love God's Word, you will take the time it requires to search it and dig into it. It will do amazing things in your life. Reading God's Word is like planting seeds of hope, joy, and security in our hearts. As you read Bible, you will come across simple and clear truths that you understand and try to live by. You will also come across truths that you might not understand at that moment, and that's ok. The Holy Spirit will help you understand the Bible step by step. The Bible will let you see yourself for who you really are and this world for what it really is — both the good and the bad.

Many people have died to get the Bible into your hands today. It was not always available to everyone. Even today, there are places where the Bible is not allowed or hasn't yet been brought. You should treasure the Bible and take the chance to study it daily for as long as you live. Bible is a big book, so you won't be able to read it all in one day. But, you will continue learning from the Bible even if you read a little every day until you are very old. The Bible is such an excellent book! You can reread it many times throughout your life and still be learning something new from it! We should do what the Bible tells us to do and share with others what we learn from God's Word.

New word: Search – to look carefully for something in an attempt to find something.

Questions to ask:

1. Can reading the Bible do amazing things in your life?
2. Will you be able to understand everything you read at once?
3. Are there any places in the world today where people don't have the Bible?

Read and discuss

Acts 8:26-35 (Christ is preached to an Ethiopian through Philip).

Let's ask God to help us study, understand and obey God's Word.

Dear God, please help us store Your Word in our hearts, so we can have wisdom and know how to live. Please bring the Bible to all parts of the world in every language, so more people can know about You. Amen.

35

SPIRITUAL ARMOR

"Put on the whole armor of God,
that you may be able to stand against the wiles of the devil."
Ephesians 6:11

Every day as your day begins, you need to put on all of the spiritual armor of God. Army soldiers wear special clothing that protects them for whatever task they have ahead of them. There is also spiritual armor for every Christian to help you live a victorious life! This armor is very awesome; it's invisible but powerful. The Belt of Truth is to help you remember the truth you know about God and to help you live an honest life. The enemy likes to fight using lies, and sometimes his lies sound like truth. This Belt of Truth will help defeat Satan's lies. The Breastplate of Righteousness is to protect your heart from Satan's accusations. It is Jesus's righteousness that covers and protects you. There are also Shoes of the Gospel. Satan tries to place difficulties in your path, but in Jesus's strength you can walk forward obeying God and telling the Good News to others. The Shield of Faith will protect you from Satan's arrows of temptations and doubts about God and about yourself. There is also a Helmet of Salvation that protects the head. It gives your mind peace because your sins are forgiven, and you have eternal life in Jesus. And the last is the Sword of the Spirit, which is the Word of God – your Bible. Jesus used this weapon when Satan tempted Him in the wilderness. God's Word is powerful because it is the truth, and that is why it is so important to study it. So, how can you put on this full armor of God? All these pieces of the armor are found in your relationship with Jesus. Give yourself daily to Him in prayer as you begin your day.

New word: Victory – winning a battle, overcoming an enemy.

Questions to ask:
1. When should you put on all of the armor of God?
2. Can you name the six pieces of the armor of God?
3. How can you put on the full armor of God?

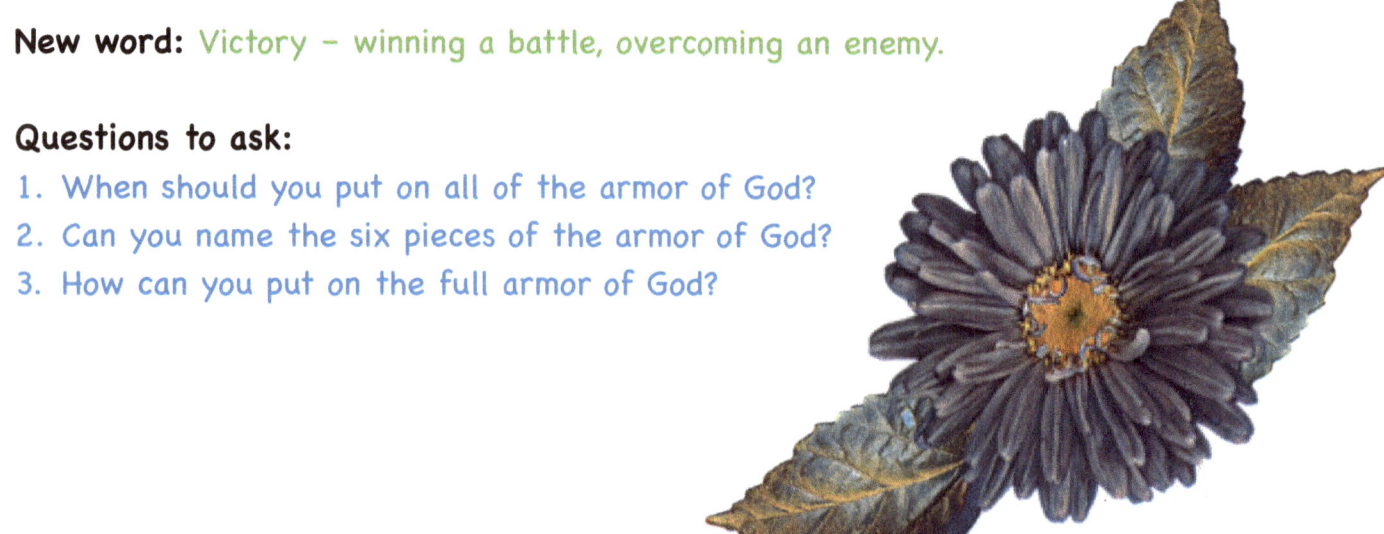

Read and discuss

Ephesians 6:10-18 (The whole armor of God).

Let's thank God for giving you everything you need to have victory over the enemy.
Dear God, thank You for the protection You give us, so we can stand against the devil. Help me put on all of Your armor every morning and help me to follow You as You lead Your army. Amen.

36

THE CHURCH

"But you are a chosen generation, a royal priesthood, a holy nation, His own special people, that you may proclaim the praises of Him who called you out of darkness into His marvelous light."
1 Peter 2:9

As a Christian, you need a relationship with other Christians to help you grow. And, other Christians need you too! Living a Christian life includes belonging to a church. Church is not a building where people meet; church is the people themselves! A church can meet in a beautiful building, in a small home or even in the forest. The church is very important. God has always wanted to have people for Himself. Long ago, God chose the nation of Israel to follow Him. Today, all of God's people are a part of His church. While Jesus was on earth, He said that He will build His church. The church began when the Holy Spirit came into the lives of Christians on the day of Pentecost. This shows us that God, Jesus and the Holy Spirit are involved in the life of the church. God has called everyone who has accepted Jesus as their Lord and Savior into His church. These are people from different places and even those who lived in different times; those who lived before you and those who might live after you. Just like in your body you have different body parts; every member of God's church makes up the body of Christ. Your hand is different from your foot, but you need them both. People in our church are different from each other, but we need everyone! God gives Christians the ability to work as one body even though we have so many differences.

When the church began, different people who might have been enemies for a long time became united in the body of Christ. Those who would not speak to one another now can come together to worship God! There is no perfect church with perfect people. The church is a real place with real people who still have struggles.

New word: Member – someone who has joined a particular group.

Questions to ask:
1. Do you need a relationship with other Christians and do they need you?
2. Does the church, the body of Christ, have different parts?
3. Is church a perfect place with perfect people?

Read and discuss
Psalm 122:1-9 (The joy of going to the house of the Lord).

Let's thank God for making His church and ask Him to unify us.

Dear God, thank You for all of the different kinds of people in the church. Thank You for a church that can never be defeated because You have made it! Help me understand the reason for Christ's church. Teach me how to love and serve the Christians in my church. Help us become more united with each other as we serve You. Amen.

YOUR SPIRITUAL FAMILY

"Do not rebuke an older man, but exhort him as a father, younger men as brothers, older women as mothers, younger women as sisters, with all purity."
1 Timothy 5:1-2

The church is your spiritual family. Your physical family is not perfect, and neither is your spiritual family. But, if you are a strong, healthy family, then you'll know how to work through difficulties and differences. Some people might be unhappy no matter what you do; others may be unkind. At times it might be hard to find an answer that will make everyone happy because we all come from different backgrounds and have different preferences. Still, Christians are to go to one another if there is a problem. You are not supposed to gossip or go around telling others about a problem you have with someone else. God doesn't want us to complain or speak badly about other people. Forgive when you have been hurt and love others despite their differences. The church is one family, and we are planning to spend eternity together in heaven. So, we should learn how to work things out with love. Everyone makes mistakes. We are all learning and growing.

Most of your spiritual growth is going to happen through your relationships with other believers. Each one of us and what we do in the body of Christ has more importance than we realize. In a brick wall, every brick is an important part of the wall. If you take one brick out, it will create a hole in the wall. It takes a lot of bricks to make a wall. One brick, no matter how good, cannot make a brick wall. In the same way, we need all of us together to build the church.

New word: Forgive – to stop blaming someone or feeling angry at him or her.

Questions to ask:
1. If there is a problem in your family, what should you do?
2. Should you forgive when you have been hurt and love others if they are different than you?
3. Is who we are and what we do in the body of Christ important?

Read and discuss
Philemon 1:1-16 (Paul pleas Philemon for Onesimus, his runaway slave).

Let's thank God for making us His family and ask Him to help us show the world His love.

Dear God, thank You for every person who makes up Your church. Help us to love one another well, so the world can see Your love through us. Amen.

38

THE CHURCH'S ASSIGNMENT

"For as we have many members in one body,
but all the members do not have the same function,
so we, being many, are one body in Christ,
and individually members of one another."
Romans 12:4-5

What is the church supposed to do? The first church in Jerusalem met with each other every day to be taught by the apostles. They had fellowship together, praised God by their words and actions, prayed together, and took the Lord's Supper together. They sold what they had to meet the needs of others, and they saw God doing great miracles. God's power was known in the first church. Believers where kind, honest, and unified; the leaders had Jesus's character. More and more people came to Jesus because of all the good they saw happening in the church; they wanted to be a part of it. This is how they grew spiritually and glorified God.

We should also continue to grow spiritually and bring glory to God's name. We do that when we invite people to come to church, and they give their life to Jesus. You grow spiritually and glorify God when you have fellowship with other Christians: worshipping together, praying and helping them in their need. When others in the church have a need, it means you have a need too. That is what it means to share each other's burdens. This is one of the reasons why we give money to meet the needs of others. Jesus said that others would see that we are Christians because of the love that we have for each other.

There are a lot of things you can do at church like being a preacher, a Sunday school teacher, a person who plans activities, the cashier or someone who sings in the choir. There are also things you can do outside of the church like being a missionary or an evangelist. God's church has a lot of work to do, and every member is called to serve in the body of Christ. That's the beauty of church: we can be strong together and learn from one another.

New word: Fellowship – a group of people meeting together to practice a shared goal.

Questions to ask:
1. How can a church glorify God and help its members grow spiritually?
2. How will others know that we are Christians?
3. Is every member called to serve?

Read and discuss
John 1:43-51 (Philip called Nathanael to Jesus).

Let's thank God for using us as His hands and feet to reach the world.
Dear God, thank You for using Your church to care for others and to bring more people into Your family. Help Your church go into the entire world and make believers, baptizing them in Your name, and teaching them to do what You have taught us to do. Amen.

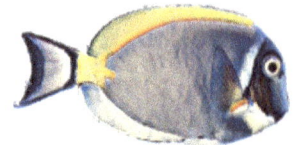

39

BAPTISM

"Therefore we were buried with Him through baptism into death, that just as Christ was raised from the dead by the glory of the Father, even so we also should walk in newness of life."
Romans 6:4

Before Jesus went up to heaven, He told His disciples to go and tell everybody about Him and to baptize all who believe in the name of the Father, the Son and the Holy Spirit. When you wash your dirty hands, you can see the change right away. But, it is hard to see the change that happens on the inside of you when you repent, ask for forgiveness for your sins, and give your life to Jesus.

Baptism is a physical picture to the world of what happened in someone's spiritual life when they became a Christian. It is an illustration of their repentance, forgiveness and new life. People being baptized are publicly saying that they believe in God and want to give their lives to Him. During baptism, when people are going down into the water, it means that Jesus forgave their sins and put those sins to death. When they come up out of the water, it means that these people are spiritually cleansed, added to the body of Christ, and living a brand-new life. Baptized people have openly identified themselves with Jesus and with other Christians. They have said that they belong together with Jesus and with other Christians.

People being baptized are making a promise to serve God for the rest of their life. They enter a covenant with God through water baptism. This is similar to a man and a woman who enter a covenant with each other as they make their promises during their wedding ceremony. Their marriage covenant lasts until death, but God's covenant through water baptism lasts forever.

New word: Identify – indicate who or what someone is.

Questions to ask:
1. Who told Jesus's disciples to go tell everybody about Jesus and to baptize all those who believe?
2. Baptism is a physical picture for who?
3. Baptized people openly identified themselves with whom?

Read and discuss
Acts 16:25-34 (The Philippian jailer saved).

Let's thank God for putting to death our sinful old way of life and for giving us new life.
Dear God, thank You for giving us a new life and for letting us show our promise to You through baptism. Please bring more people to accept this new life that You offer them. Help me to be faithfully involved in Your church. And, thank You for everything You are doing in the world through Your church. Amen.

40

THE LORD'S SUPPER

"And when He had given thanks, He broke it and said,
"Take, eat; this is My body which is broken for you;
do this in remembrance of Me."
In the same manner He also took the cup after supper, saying,
"This cup is the new covenant in My blood.
This do, as often as you drink it, in remembrance of Me."
For as often as you eat this bread and drink this cup,
you proclaim the Lord's death till He comes."
1 Corinthians 11:24-26

Passover was a holiday that the Hebrew people celebrated every year by eating a special meal of lamb, herbs and bread. This was to remind them of how God delivered them from slavery to the Egyptians and how He protected them from death. Passover was the night when Hebrews placed the blood of a lamb on the doorposts of their homes. Those who did not have blood on the doorposts lost their firstborn son. This was a sign of the blood of Jesus that was going to be given for our deliverance.

Jesus began "The Lord's Supper" at the end of the Passover meal; He and His disciples ate on the night He was betrayed. At that meal, Jesus told the disciples what He was about to do on the cross for them and the whole world. He told them of the covenant or promise God was going to fulfill between Himself and the world: that those who believe in Jesus will be saved from their sins.

The Lord's Supper, or often known as Communion, is a very important fellowship with Jesus and with other believers. We remember all that Jesus did for us as we take the Lord's Supper. It is a physical reminder of a spiritual truth: how He suffered and died for our sins and for us. Communion allows Christians to share in Jesus's sacrifice as we take a piece of bread and a sip of wine. We feel His great love for us and for everyone else having the Lord's Supper in the same room and all over the world. Like the Hebrews, we too have experienced a day of deliverance from spiritual death and slavery to sin. We have a lot to remember and be thankful for.

New word: Covenant – an agreement between two or more people.

Questions to ask:
1. Who held the first Communion?
2. When Jesus died on the cross, what promise was God able to fulfill?
3. What do we remember as we take the Lord's Supper?

Read and discuss
Matthew 26:26-30 (Jesus and the disciples have the last supper).

Let's thank God for the opportunity to express our devotion to Christ when we are baptized and when we eat the Lord's Supper together.

Dear God, thank You for giving us reminders of how You freed us from sin and death. Thank You for your Son Jesus dying on the cross for us. Thank You for his broken body, which brings us healing. Thank You for his perfect blood, which washes away our sins. Amen.

THE END TIMES

*"Men's hearts failing them from fear and the expectation
of those things which are coming on the earth,
for the powers of the heavens will be shaken.
Then they will see the Son of Man
coming in a cloud with power and great glory."*
Luke 21:26-27

Bible tells us that this world will pass away. All that you see around you will come to an end. Jesus will come again to take His church! God made the heavens and the earth for His glory. Everything praised God in the beginning before sin came and spoiled His beautiful creation. But, everything will praise Him again one day soon.
One of Jesus's disciples John was sent away to a lonely island. Some men were trying to stop John from telling others about Jesus. While John was there alone, he saw a vision of the events that are going to happen. John wrote them in a book called Revelation, which you can find in the Bible. Some of the events he saw were terrible. All the wickedness and evil in the world was punished including people who did not love and serve God. After these horrible events, John also saw wonderful revelations: a New Heaven and a New Earth. He saw a beautiful city coming down from heaven, which was going to be the New Jerusalem.
The way things are right now will change. The world will be full of evil and God will bring judgement for every bad thing that is done. There will be a very hard time ahead for us, but God will be with His faithful people to help them. When your family is going on a trip, your parents pack all the things they might need. But, how can you prepare for the days ahead? You can prepare by staying alert, listening to God's voice, and living a holy life. Say no to sin but say yes to prayer, reading the Bible, and serving others. Try to please the Lord in everything you do and say. God will always care for those that love Him.

New word: Revelation – to make something known that was previously unknown or secret.

Questions to ask:
1. How do we know that this world will pass away?
2. When John was on the island, what did he see in a vision?
3. Will God help those who are faithful to Him in the hard times ahead?

Read and discuss
2 Peter 3:10-13 (The Day of the Lord).

Let's thank God for telling you what will happen in the future. Let's ask God to help us trust that He is in control instead of worrying about things.

Dear God, we believe You know the future. Thank You for telling us about the New Heaven and about Your glorious victory. Help me to live a holy life and not worry about the hard times ahead. I know that You will prepare me and guide me. Amen.

42

IF I DIE

*"Behold, I tell you a mystery: We shall not all sleep,
but we shall all be changed."*
1 Corinthians 15:51

All of us think about what death will be like. Jesus's disciples and friends hoped to see Jesus come back from heaven while they were still living, but they died. God thought it was best that way, and maybe God will think it is best for you to die too before Jesus comes again. But, you don't have to be afraid. Your body is only a house where your spirit lives. If you are a God's child, your spirit – the real you – will go right to heaven and be with Jesus. There is no waiting time. But, your body will be buried in a grave and will wait for the wonderful day when Jesus will give you a new body. Death will only take you from one place to another. You will still remain the same person. But now you will be present with the Lord. You don't become an angel when you die. Angels and people have always been different creations. Those who are in Christ, they are sons and daughters of the living God! The angels serve God and His children.
Christians from all different times are now with the Lord in heaven. Their bodies wait for the resurrection, but their spirit is with the Lord! You may be happy here on earth because God has given you so many good things, but to be with Jesus in heaven is so much better! Apostle Paul writes in Philippians 1:23 "For I am hard-pressed between the two, having a desire to depart and be with Christ, which is far better." If you have troubles here on earth, you know they will last only a little while. In heaven, God promises that there will be no more sickness, sadness, pain or death. You can be happy as you look ahead to the wonderful things that will come when you join Jesus in heaven.

New word: Bury – to put a dead body underground.

Questions to ask:
1. If you are God's child and you die before Jesus returns, where will your spirit go?
2. What will happen to your body when you die?
3. Is life better on earth or with Jesus in heaven?

Read and discuss
Ecclesiastes 12:7 (The dust and spirit).

Let's thank God that you don't have to be afraid of dying if you have accepted Jesus. You are just traveling through this world, and your heart waits for that day when Jesus will gloriously return.

Dear God, thank You for promising to take my spirit into heaven when I die. My heart wants to see You and be with You. Help me live my life for You while I am still on this earth. Amen.

43

HEAVEN

*"But now they desire a better,
that is, a heavenly country.
Therefore God is not ashamed
to be called their God,
for He has prepared a city for them."*
Hebrews 11:16

There's still a lot we don't know about heaven, but God has told us just enough to help us while we're on earth. We'll know the rest when we get there. However, we do know that heaven is a perfect place. It is God's dwelling place: God's home and the home of those who choose to follow Jesus with their lives while still on earth. It's a place of never ending joy, safety, and strong relationships. A place where all of your needs will be met.

On your good days and on your bad days, remember that there is more to this life than what you see on earth. Earth is not the best that it can be, and God tells us that things will be much better in heaven.

Bible tells us that everyone will stand before God. Two different judgments will take place. One judgment is for those who did not believe in Jesus, where they will hear if they will be in heaven. Those who don't enter heaven will have the final punishment of being separated from God and His goodness forever.

The other judgment is for those who believed in Jesus and made Him Lord of their life. This is a judgment of reward! You will stand in the presence of all, and all of your works will be tested. The fire will check the quality of everything you have done, and you will be rewarded for the things you did that survive the fire. What could those things be? They must be the truly important things. For example, the people that have come to know Christ because of you, any Christlike character that you have developed, when you cared for the needy and the unnoticed people, when you suffered because of your faith in Jesus, when you prayed for others and made sacrifices in the name of Jesus. God will reward every time you act, think or speak in a Christlike way. Those are the things that will survive the fire, and you will be rewarded for them.

New word: Reward – something that is given to someone for his or her effort and achievement.

Questions to ask:
1. Is heaven a perfect place?
2. Will everyone stand before God at one of the two judgments?
3. What things will God reward you for?

Read and discuss
Revelation 21:1-27
(All things made new).

Let's thank God for the desire that we have in our hearts for our heavenly home.

Dear God,
Thank You for creating me to spend eternity with You. Help me to use my gifts and abilities to live for that which lasts and not just to build a good life for myself in this world.
Amen.

44

HELL

*"The devil, who deceived them, was cast into the lake of fire
and brimstone where the beast and the false prophet are.
And they will be tormented day and night forever and ever."
Revelation 20:10*

Once this world is destroyed, living separate from God will no longer be possible. That is why hell was originally created for Satan and his demons as a place of separation from God. Satan will be in hell, not to rule but to be locked up and punished/tortured for what he has done.
Hell is a place totally separated from God. There is no love, no kindness, no forgiveness, no beauty and no light. There are no parties or friends. It's a place of endless regret; a place of death with no rest and no second chances. We wouldn't wish for anyone to be there, and neither does God. Those who reject Jesus as the Son of God and their Savior decide to live separate from God in this life and in the eternal life. God doesn't send people to hell. People do that to themselves because of their choice to live separated from God. Everyone who is in hell is there by their own choice.
We should be very thankful for Jesus our Savior who saves us from the pain of hell! If you have friends or family who have not yet accepted Jesus as their Savior, pray for their salvation. Ask God to give you boldness and words to tell them that Jesus came to forgive their sins if they turn to Him.

New word: Torment – severe pain and suffering.

Questions to ask:
1. What will happen to Satan in hell?
2. Is hell a place totally separated from God?
3. Do people end up in hell by their own choice?

Read and discuss
Luke 16:19-29 (The Rich Man and Lazarus).

Let's thank God for how great our salvation truly is through Jesus, and ask Him to save people in our lives.
Dear God, thank You for saving me from a scary and dark place like hell. Help me live a holy life. Help me tell others about Your love, so they can accept Your Son Jesus and live in peace with You in heaven forever. Amen.

45

THE SECOND COMING OF JESUS

"For the Lord Himself will descend from heaven with a shout,
with the voice of an archangel, and with the trumpet of God.
And the dead in Christ will rise first."
1 Thessalonians 4:16

Jesus is going to come back just like how He went up to heaven when He was on a mountain with His disciples. It has been many years since Jesus went to heaven, and He has not come back yet. No one except the Heavenly Father knows the exact day of Jesus's coming. But, we know it's getting closer. There are some things that Jesus said would happen before His return. Earthquakes and wars will increase. There will be the biggest famine and a huge lack of food. Many people will turn away from the faith in Jesus and will make fun of it. All kinds of evil will increase. False teachers who spread lies will be very popular. But, when all the nations hear about Jesus, He will come back for us! In Matthew 24:29-31 Jesus says, "Immediately after the tribulation of those days the sun will be darkened, and the moon will not give its light; the starts will fall from heaven, and the powers of the heavens will be shaken. Then the sign of the Son of Man will appear in heaven, and then all the tribes of the earth will mourn, and they will see the Son of Man coming on the clouds of heaven with power and great glory. And He will send His angles with a great sound of a trumpet, and they will gather together His elect from the four winds, from one end of heaven to the other."
Jesus will come suddenly in the clouds and His many angles will be with Him. There will be a great shout and a trumpet will blow. All the people on earth will hear and see Jesus! Even the dead will be awakened and come out of their graves. Those who did not love Him will be very afraid, wanting to hide. But, those who love Him will be very happy because He will take them up to meet Him in the clouds. From wherever you are – at home, at school, or at play – He will take you up with Him if you belong to Him. Jesus will give all of God's children new wonderful bodies that are perfect for heaven. This world will soon be no more. That's why you should live your life for the heavenly things that will last. Jesus, who knows you best and loves you the most, has prepared a place for you in heaven. It will be the most wonderful, exciting experience in your life when He comes back for you!

New word: Return – come back to a place where you were before.

Questions to ask:
1. Does anyone know the exact day of Jesus's second coming?
2. Will everyone hear and see Jesus's second coming?
3. What will be the most wonderful, exciting experience in your life?

Read and discuss
Mark 13:3-37 (The signs of the times and the end of the age).

Let's thank God for His promise to return for you.

Dear God, thank You for promising to come back for me because You want to be with me! Help me to use my time wisely here on earth and to be ready for when You come back. Amen.